Original Face

Also from Gunpowder Press:
The Tarnation of Faust: Poems by David Case
Mouth & Fruit: Poems by Chryss Yost
Shaping Water: Poems by Barry Spacks

Original Face

Poems

Jim Peterson

Gunpowder Press • Santa Barbara
2015

© 2015 Jim Peterson

Published by Gunpowder Press
David Starkey, Editor
PO Box 60035
Santa Barbara, CA 93160-0035

Cover art: Jim Muehlemann
Back cover photo: Harriet Peterson

ISBN-13: 978-0-9916651-5-0

www.gunpowderpress.com

I dedicate this book to Harriet—
my teacher, my student, my lover, my best and most intimate friend,
my Eve, my heroine…

With gratitude to my many poet friends
who helped me with astute readings of these poems
leading to stronger and stronger drafts.

I especially want to thank my 'poultry' group—Laura-Gray Street,
Bunny Goodjohn, and Gary Dop—for their rigorous workshopping
of many of these poems.

Acknowledgements

Poems in this collection appeared in the following publications (sometimes in earlier versions):

Burnt District: "Migration," "Lust at the Lecture on Modernist Painters"
Cave Wall: "Woodcreek 1977," "Original Face," "The Long Roads," "The Prisoner's Dance"
Chariton Review: "Asleep"
Connecticut Review: "The Captain"
Greensboro Review: "Second Sight"
Hampden-Sydney Review: "Who Knows," "The Note"
Lady Jane's Miscellany: "Las Vegas"
Platte Valley Review (online): "First Sight"
Poem: "Because I Could," "Near"
Poetry International: "Things Would Be Different: An Aubade to My Cat"
Poetry Northwest: "One Shot"
Salt Fork Review: "The Vein in a Child's Temple"
Shenandoah: "The Map to Her Place"
South Dakota Review: "Rain of Bulls," "A Way of Flying," "The Marriage," "The Giant's Dream of Love," "Love Song of the Maintenance Engineer"
Southern Poetry Review: "No News"
Sugar House Review: "Black"
Texas Review: "One of Us"
The Resolution of Eve, a chapbook published by Finishing Line Press: "The Present Moment," "Circus Queen," "Other Laws for the People," "Rain of Bulls," "A Way of Flying," "The Kidnapping Horse," "The Marriage," "The Giant's Dream of Love," "The Blanket," "Men and Women in Sacks"

Contents

Prologue: Because I Could 11

Black Dirt

First Sight 15
The Map to Her Place 16
Who Knows 18
No News 20
The Captain 21
One Shot 23
The Long Roads 24
Spit 26
Planting Season 28
Black 29
Winchester 30
Intersection 31

The Drawstring from Within

Rain of Bulls 35
The Present Moment 36
The Kidnapping Horse 37
Circus Queen 39
The Marriage 40
A Way of Flying 41
The Giant's Dance of Love 43
The Blanket 45
Men and Women in Sacks 47
Other Laws for the People 49

Flesh Among the Ferns

Love Song of the Maintenance Engineer 53
Lust at the Lecture on Modernist Painters 58

Nameable Strangers

Second Sight   65
Trouble   67
The Vein in a Child's Temple   69
One of Us   71
The Prisoner's Dance   73
Your Eyes When You Walk Out on Me   74
Woodcreek 1977   76
Asleep   78
Near   81
Things Would Be Different: An Aubade to My Cat   82
Original Face   84
Down and Up   87
The Grip   90
Las Vegas   92
The Note   94
The Syllable   97
Epilogue: Migration   98

Every she is an Eve. Every he is an Adam.
        Every Adam is an Eve. Every Eve is an Adam.

— A friend

What is your original face before your parents were born?

— Zen koan

Prologue: Because I Could

She said Van Gogh
and told me to translate
each of those explosive strokes
into a letter or word
and I tried, hammering
the thick museum air
into a sentence
like a rope ladder climbing
into the canopied heart of the artist.

She said Chagall
and told me to break the code
of those curves and undulations
stalling in air like dreams
above a sleeping face,
and I tried, drawing the raw light
into the convoluted path
of a lone, grazing horse
in a rolling field of grass.

We walked outside and she said stars,
so I took a sturdy conjurer's stance
and called them forth
because on this night I could,
each one of them an immortal wound
bleeding into our small laughter.
The leaves fell from sheer exhaustion—
how long they had labored to remain upright—
what a blaze they made beneath our feet.

Black Dirt

First Sight

She pretends to read an old book
while her eyes sneak a glance
of each face in the room.
But what she really believes in
shimmers in the air around her
like a spray of individual beads
stunned by the sun.
No husky insurance salesman
can turn her head
except to notice the particular
coloration of his feathers
in sunlight, or the way
his nape rises at the scent
of a potential mate.
She looks at me looking at her
and her eyes go back to words,
her smile so faint only the faith
of a man makes it true.
No rusty instrument of fate
is too old or too trivial
for her. She can pluck the dolphin
from the depth of any day's desire.
She can roll the last crumb
of sweetness
beneath her thumb for hours.
The naked foot adrift above her sandal
is the moon of this system.
How do I know?
I was born when everything else
was born, way back
when those original molecules
got their first good
look at one another.

The Map to Her Place

His lenses stare at him from the bar,
warping the scarred shellac of the wood.
Knotholes spin into dusk,
ashtrays reel in the listless light.
The waitress wears a tank top and he

can't take his eyes off her bare arms,
her perfect navel above beltless jeans.
A blue vine tattoo with serrated leaves creeps
down her forearm and between her fingers.
She smiles at him, says her name is Angela,

wipes off tables, sweeps debris into piles.
Nothing escapes her, not the swirl
of thumbprints, not even the cupped residue
of voices on spoons. He says he's alone
for the first time in a hundred years,

says to call him Gary, wants to know
if there's a decent motel in walking distance.
She brings him a plate of fries, sits down
and lights a Winston. She pours him
another bourbon and draws him a map

to her place. Later, not finding a room,
he seeks her landmarks—the blinking neon
of an upstairs pool hall, an old fedora
cocked rakishly on a school ground flagpole—
following into a neighborhood where boys

play war on the streets and women
draw hearts and stars in the palms of their hands.
When he finds her place, he sits
on her front stoop and waits. At 2 a.m.
she nudges him awake with her bare foot.

How did she know he would lie all night
on her couch bathed in the TV's pale light?
How did she know he would sleep like a child?

Who Knows

You'd wait all day to bring out that old
harmonica wrapped in a plastic bag,
hidden in the high crotch of an ancient
oak. Nobody else wants that thing, I'd say,
but you'd sneak around anyway, cupping it
in your palm like a sacred egg. Those long
notes ascending like the whine of a handsaw
hurled me back to the ten years we worked
for Seymore, building matchbox houses
on the outskirts of town, until you got
the bright idea of stealing his copper wiring.
When Seymore caught us he didn't call the cops —
just hired that goon Phil to chase us out of town,
firing his .38 at the sky. Before that it was
high school, meaning Brianna, who said yes
to Seymore before you could make your pitch.
Whenever we got back to Pelion, we headed
straight for the park, pulled down that rusty
old harp, and somehow you made it play.
We had no food, no money, no place to go,
it was getting dark and still you'd play,
rain making little waterfalls off the brim
of your hat, until you'd had your fill of what
we'd seen and done in twenty years. Not enough
jazzy parts, I'd complain, meaning women.
Didn't I do everything you asked? I joined
your vow against all forms of labor, except
those times hunger forced us to take up tools
building lean-to's and cattle sheds, working
mostly in the Carolinas. You loved waking up
to those damp fields, the dumb eyes of cows,
sparrows quibbling overhead. But I know

you preferred thievery. One August
in Chicago, twelve inches of rain in two days
flooded the underground parking lots.
We were forced to the streets for five days
and nights without sleep. Every pawnshop
and strip club was a shrine for something
you couldn't find. The girls would come over
to you, bad as you looked, and sit in your lap
to talk about their c-sections and how they'd
kicked the habit, and how their father'd called them
Tawny and the name had stuck, though they
were really Elizabeth. Or maybe you always
found it, going on about Tawny's fine eyes,
the healing power of her hands, her mystical
turn of mind. I'd like to ask you how come
I saw her as just another worn-out whore,
how come that old wooden horse in Pinky's
Pawn and Dine was never beautiful to me
like it was to you. And I'd like to ask where
you disappeared to one night when the booze
was good and you were seeing right through
everything, even the malamute tied outside Jake's
that tried to take off part of your leg. Even me—
you said you could see right through to the bones,
and by the end through them until I wasn't there.
Maybe it was me that disappeared. All I know
is that I turned over every cardboard box and tin strip
for a month until I had to leave with the cold wind
coming off the lake. It took me another hard month
to get to this warm November in Pelion. I found
your father in the nursing home, but he acted like
he'd never had a son. I know you'd have left
a message if you got here first, but all I can find
is the plastic bag and that flaky harp. I wipe it off
with spit and sleeve, and blow this sour note.

No News

I like the tight cylinder of a newspaper
and keep it intact, maneuvering the rubber
band to read a line. I'm pulled into the curved
space of a photograph where imagination
completes the scene and the caption.

My methods save me time and a lot of pain.
I don't let myself think about much
except that smoldering potion I'm preparing
for you, complete with chocolate ice cream
on the side and watermelon waiting in the fridge.

See, the phone has lapsed and the street
disappears. I ought to go back to bagging
groceries, which is a study of hands.
Or maybe pizza delivery, where the brain
becomes a map sprouting avenues.

That could be the way to rediscover the way
back to you, since the potion misting my window
has done nothing but bore the birds. Soon I'll
be sliding into some immovable posture,
having drunk the potion myself. I can't

invite you back to this place. My neighbor's
dogs bark too loud at everything that moves.
Only the trees hold time and space together.
The tabby you didn't take with you keeps
landing on the outer sill and squinting in.

The Captain

Last night she found the mask.
Tonight she put it on, the tear
revealing part of her own lip.
She did this knowing she was alone,
standing before her mirror,

sea captain's head on a woman's body
with a woman's small eyes
peering from beneath its brow.
Her father wore it to a Halloween party,
laughing on his way out the door

that it scared even him when he
looked in the mirror. God knows
why she kept it all these years.
Her husband hates the mask, but knows
he cannot throw it away.

She likes to feel the rubber tight
across her skin where her father's skin
had been, likes to feel his grin
beneath the outer grimace, wants to know
in her own eyes that power

of the Commander shining through.
The mirror fills with spinning lights
and dancing masqueraders, the dead
salesman himself telling her
what it was like on the dirty road

to dirty towns. Perfect in his captain's
white and navy blue, he never takes
his eyes away from her. It's late
when she crawls into bed
beside her sleeping husband.

She remembers the captain's silhouette
in the door of her room,
his salesman's soft clean hands,
the smell of his breath
through rubber lips.

One Shot

The man did not choose this dream,
this road tumbling over hills,
wheel thrumming in his palms.
The navigator snaps her map

and squints into red and black lines.
In the back seat a small boy reads aloud
from the book of conjured artifacts.
"Petroglyph," he says. "Arrowhead."

The radio grows songless as an old tire.
The navigator chants the names of towns
and historical sites. "Pompey's Pillar,"
she says. "Butte." The boy traces

an elk that stands on its hind legs
holding an ornate shield. The landscape
warps, a rumpled bedspread snapped
into flatness. "Get dressed," she laughs,

"you've got just one shot at this day."
The man watches her hands smooth
away those last lines, every direction
that could be made or unmade.

The Long Roads

She takes down the laundry,
studies a pair of pink socks
far too small for her
that she washes again and again
so as not to forget
what was never finally given.
She stares beyond the split-rail fence
overtaken by honeysuckle
into the rutted dirt road.

A child hides among the oval leaves
and white trumpet flowers,
sweat running down her back.
She can see the woman's blue sneakers,
wonders why the woman has grown
so still above her, fears
the sound of her own voice,
her own breath,
buried as she is
among the praying mantises.

A pickup passes and the woman waves,
turning back at last to the line, away
from the presence she feels
dreaming in the leaves around her.
Her man will come home again
and they will have their dinner.
The night will crawl out
from the roots of great maples and oaks

through their windows and into their bed,
into the fallow and fertile fields,
down the long roads
that lead to all of their kind,
even that curious child
resting deep in the vine.

Spit

A woman sits on the gray floorboards
of a front porch. A morning wind blows
over the broken rail. A fallow field stretches
like a long day to a dark green line of trees.

The woman crosses her legs Indian style,
blue shift sliding halfway up her thighs,
hair wild around her long, angular face.
She turns an old boot in her hands, unthreads

the black leather lace and places it beside her.
She breaks gray clods of mud from the tread
with her fingers, casts about with her eyes
for the mate, finds it beneath the rocker,

removes the lace and lays it next to the other.
She claps the two soles together and debris
flies, scatters in slivers and flakes across
the floor and down the front steps. The earth

of a distant, high meadow collects in her hair,
falls around her like shards of an ancient vase.
The wildflowers she has seen there—white
and blue and red—stand out to her now,

each one of them unique and worthy of a face.
The rain that maintained them for a while
drifts now over some dark city to the south.
Everything descends into this worthiness,

everything looks back at her from where it is.
Mindfully she drives the two boots together
for a long time—for a thousand years it seems—
until nothing else can fly away. Still,

the hard slap of those boots fills the morning,
fills this almost empty house, even the room
where a man sleeps beneath pillows and covers
in the darkness of drawn shades and a closed door.

And when she stops, the silence of fields and roads,
of faraway towns and cities leaning to the sun
still low in the sky—pours in through the rails
and fills the porch. Fills the woman who sits

in that silence as if she were holding her breath
at the bottom of a deep pond. Finally, she breathes,
pulls out a red handkerchief, shapes it just right,
spits, and buffs the boots raw and clean.

Planting Season

She has black dirt on her face,
like she's taken a fall, but I see no blood
and she walks okay. Whatever
happened, her eyes are full of zoom.
She sits at a table near mine
and orders a beer. Black dirt crumbles
from her hands when she tilts the bottle
back. She lets it gush, lets it
wobble and gurgle down her throat.
When she looks at me, her eyes
bore two holes in the part of my brain
that is heart. She spits, but not
because of what she's looking at.
It's that black dirt in her mouth.
She smiles, grabs her bottle, sloshes beer
on the loose circle of soil around her,
sashays over for a visit,
captures the chair across from mine,
and lowers the heels of her bare feet,
smudged with black dirt,
onto the table. "I hope you like
black dirt," she says. I make a grin
with as much black dirt in it
as I can muster. "Oh yes," I say.

Black

He knows how to tell three stories
in his sky-scraping language:
you know, the one about making the world
out of barbed wind and solar dust—
and the one about calling forth rascal man
and rascal woman from the black mud—
and the one about jumping from some cliff
to catch a cold current into the canyon
so black with its own inner shadow
the river becomes only the sound of rushing water.

And he is blacker than the black dirt
you can still find in those creek-running
hollers deep in the woods.
More the black of a beetle's back
in a country where the trees still grow so tall
that when they disappear in the sky
they are black and moving
like the crow in your memory's eye.

Winchester

How grand it was when he was four
to play our animal games under the chairs.

When he was eight, he was still mine.
We walked in the woods with field guides
and cameras, shooting the wildflowers,
the serrated and unserrated leaves,
the Yellow Tanagers and the Grackles.

When he was twelve, he did not need
a mother to teach him to break the gun down
and put it back together again. Did not
want a mother to show him how to press
the stock against his cheek, how to hold
a buck in his sight while squeezing
the trigger. It took a man, my husband,
to demonstrate with his knife the art
of gutting a deer in the field, the art
of taking the head as one more trophy.

When he was eighteen, they brought him
back to me in a box, face so ruined
I couldn't look at him—terrible
accident his father said, placing the boy's
beautiful Winchester on his empty bed.

Intersection

I scratch an old tick bite on my left shoulder.
The trail meanders among tall skinny pines

and over fallen trunks. I pick up a stick
and whip the air before my face to scare away

the biting flies. A year ago right here a scream
made me hunker near the ground. Twenty yards

farther on I found the writhing deer, blood
staining her flank around the arrow buried

in her flesh, hooves kicking up the dry
needles, decomposing leaves. Here too, once,

she put her arms around my waist and pressed
her breasts against my back, whispered in my ear

let's build a fire. We lay down on our spread jackets,
listened to the wild laughter of the pileated woodpecker

at the intersection of these two trails where
almost no one ever walks but us. Her fingers

traced the fresh stitches on my thigh. A man wearing
camouflage appeared beside the deer, pistol

drawn against her temple. He shifted his tobacco knob
from one cheek to the other, and pulled the trigger.

The Drawstring from Within

A sequence of poems based on
The Disparates, or, The Proverbios
by Francisco Goya y Lucientes

Rain of Bulls

They plunge through space spread-
eagled, eyes stretched so open wide

the lids may split, tails askew, horns
ripping the air like knife blades in a sheet.

The great muscles of their haunches
quiver as if to transform into wings.

But what good would flight do them
in a place that knows no north or south

or east or west? What cloud coalesced
to create them? What earth awaits their seed?

The Present Moment

To her right she holds hands with a man
whose elbow is a laughing face, and who
himself holds hands with a line
of triple-faced gawkers and weepers
and sly glancers.

To her left she holds hands with a man
who bends into a gracious bow to the world,
tipping his white hat like a suitor.
With him stands another, hollow-eyed,
right hand thumb-cocked and finger

pointed like a gun, shouting some lecture.
She braces against the man to her right—
her eyes round with fear.
Behind her, a great eagle rises
against the night sky—dark tumult

of wind and wing—the one
who could remind her of her purpose.
But its voice shimmers deep within, where
she does not train her heart to listen, in this
taut moment, stretched between one man and another.

The Kidnapping Horse

What a pair you make,
your dress caught
in that stallion's
teeth, your legs
spread high above
the ground as he
rears, spins you,
bliss shining
from your back-
slung face, your eyes
dark and blind
to the outer world,
arms and hands
outstretched in empty
embrace. I would
leave you to your
rapture, but I can't take
my eyes off this
dance, his front
hooves flashing
against the dark sky,
your toes not
touching the ground.
Did he sweep you
off your feet, or
were you already
revolving around
him, the wind
to his spinning heart?
His ears prick forward

like antennae tuned
to some transmitting
center deep inside your
breast. At first glance
your body appears
out of control,
but I see that he flies you
perfectly on the axis
of his centrifugal
force. By the time
he's done, nothing
will be left of you,
nothing but the husk
of pleasure so great
no mortal man
can hope to match it.
When he finally
drops you to the
ground, you will
know no direction.
They will find you
lying here, earth
churned up around
you, tears streaking
your face, smiling
that infernal smile.
For these and so many
other reasons, my dear,
the wedding is off.

Circus Queen

I have come to see the spectacle: lithe
bodies playing fly and catch on the trapeze;
a family of elephants posturing like kings
and queens and princes; a bearded man
resting his head in the maw of a lion; acrobats
whipping like thrown knives through the air.

What I get is what I could not imagine:

On a rope strained into strong angles
by the animal's weight, a horse
floats before me like a dream
frozen in some visionary time and place.
A woman stands on its back, right foot
centered on the lacy pad for a saddle, left
foot half way up the horse's neck. She holds
long reins, but delicately, as if the slightest
touch were words of great significance in horse.
A man beside me yawns; another laughs.

Her placid eyes follow the reins down
to the spot between his ears. They prick forward.
He holds his front hooves and back hooves
one before the other, a posture no ordinary
horse could keep even on solid ground.
I stare so hard my eyes draw all the light
of evening stars around the pair, till they glow
in stillness and silence like a moonlit cloud.
No music, no drum roll, announces their beginning
or their end.

The Marriage

The woman on his back must arch her back
to conform to his, her breasts uncovered

and presented like a prayer to the sky,
her arms and hands pressed across

her midriff, her double-footed feet dangling
like wet rags in the dust. The back

of her head is truly married to his,
the half-shell of her ear the mate to his,

her dark hair growing from his scalp.
The pupils of her lidless eyes, round

and surrounded by white, stare
into the pitiless black sky. Is her mouth

agape for yawn, or scream, or howl?
But the woman on the man's back says

nothing. At his command she bends
her feet to the ground and hoists him

on her back. He smacks his lips
and prepares to doze. She

takes a heavy step, her eyes
two grey craters on a silver moon.

A Way of Flying

I am a woman, and I know I'm not
supposed to see this, this secret throng of men
above my head. They soar like vultures
in the dark sky. The light of ground fires
illuminates the pale skin of their bodies.
Are these men strapped to the underbellies

of great birds? Or are they bound to only
the hollow frames of winged machines?
Why do they get to keep this for themselves?
I want to fly, to feel the way of wings
inside of me. Among them, my own man
catches and holds for himself that grace

and lift of air, his eyes touching places
farther than I can dream. I want to soar.
They will use it only to attack their enemies.
My man would press me into the ground
to make me heavy with his son, while he
swoops low over the trees, high over

the crests of hills and floors of plains,
cruising deep through the valley of the great river.
I become still as a scrub oak, and he
doesn't see me, his face concentrated
on far ahead, the bird's eyes above his
intent on horizon, the thrust of his wings

like the song of a whip in the air. I am
a woman, lost on my shortcut home
from a day of mending clothes in the town,
the tips of my fingers numb with the press
of needles. But now that I see what I see
I want to fly more than anything I've dreamed.

I will not return to my man's house
in the village, to paths I have worn so deeply
with my feet. Alone, I will cultivate
the way of lithe feather, study the corridors
of wind—until I meet him in the air one day,
and he does not know my name.

The Giant's Dance of Love

The rapid fire of your castanets conjures
the heads of my dead mother and father
dangling like puppets beneath your arms:
my father screams; my mother gapes.
If only the boulders of your knees
didn't swing so close to me, if only

your ingratiating grin were not so fierce,
if only your squinting eyes did not focus
on mine with such wild hope, then maybe
I could forget you and live my thwarted life.
But every day you search until you find me.
You whirl around me until I see nothing

but their distorted faces, hear nothing
but their slurred voices in the thunder
of your feet against the earth. Such a promise
I had to make to break the cyclone spell
of your performance. So here I am again,
bearing the gift you asked for, in a place

where no one ventures, except the mindless
who stir this wind and light and dust
into visions like pets to warm their hearts.
You are no pet. You are the marriage
of my mother and father come back to haunt me.
I have nothing I can offer you but this,

my wife wrapped in her finest cloak, better
than any bag of silver, pleasing to the eye
and strong as the north wind. She's yours,
I don't need her any more. So tie a rope
around her neck and drag her with you,
slave to your ancient dream of love.

The Blanket

One does not expect to stumble upon
six women playing such a game, especially
on an empty plain at midnight,
the last stand of hardwood forest
a wall of cicadas and wind-stirred canopy
behind me, the tongue of trail
bright as salt in the moon.

A small spray of dust churns up
from their shoes. I tip my hat but they make
no respectful gesture of regard.
Their eyes see cleanly through me into God
knows what: insects singing in the woods
behind me perhaps, or the scarred
mind of a fox hidden among the roots.

They engage in a game I played as a child,
tossing our willing victim up in the air
from a stretched blanket, except these women
hurl the rag-doll bodies of two men
against the sky where they grow
transparent and disappear.

The women never cease
stretching and snapping the dank cloth
until some heftiness congeals there,
the woman with her back to me
crouching low with the blanket's new weight,
she and her nearest friend communing
eye to eye, while another works with a side-long
stoic gaze, another almost blocked from view.
The farthest from me, I see now, suppresses
a small smile and lets her eyes find me, engage me

with a promise...But where could man
and woman meet in this barren outpost of cracked
lake-bed, though I do not blame her for her need
or her particular choice of man.

They begin their rhythmic uplifting
of the blanket's cargo—this time a mule

and a man tumbling in a chaos of entangled limbs.
Soon enough the women sling both mule and man
against the sky where they become more cloud
than flesh, before they fade—born dead
and thrown like so much trash into greater death.

You can imagine how I would despise
the innkeeper who directed me on this path,
were it not for the promising glance
of that moonstruck woman who pulls
her heavy load in this endless game.
More flesh has taken hold of cloth
and the sweat beads above her lip.
She cannot take her eyes from me.

I step to the edge of the blanket to see her better,
moisture from the snap of it spraying my face,
her face more wet and white than any skin I've known.
Suddenly I fall beneath her feet in the mud,
more muck now than man, the carved muscles of her thighs
a rising spiral of light in a dark whorl of cave.
She unravels me, unhinges my bones, re-employs
my cells until I am lifted up and falling, lifted up
and falling, lifted up and falling, then flying
faraway into nothing that will ever speak again,
or breathe, or mate.

Men and Women in Sacks

Wrapped in loose bags, we
hop in our long procession.
We have grown almost silent,
mere squeaks and gasps, even
the fierce-eyed woman

who holds herself straight and strong.
When the last light of a long day
creeps into every crevice, I lie
hidden among clouds of dust.
Like me, the woman lingers behind,

the long line of us disappearing
on the horizon. And I see her
release the drawstring from within,
reveal her naked body which lies down
in the luminous stream flowing always

beside us. She vanishes. Minutes
later she pulls herself back onto
the bank, her wet body glinting
like a sword, and draws the husk
of her ancient bag around her.

But then she sees me, my old friend
the woman. She smiles, nods her head,
no words. And together we draw
our own maps in the sand, and together
we step out of our sacks, open

our bodies to the light and the dark
and to each other, and together
we lie down in the river
of deep currents, the cold
pouring over us, together swim, free

to find our own way home.

Other Laws for the People

We have found the elephant in her lair,
the great white crater-lake beyond her
gouged out by some ancient asteroid
or by the monumental tooth of a glacier.
Is the strangeness of this place a sign

of sacredness? or just an indication
of the loneliness of the beast? The slope
of her forehead, the ascent of her back,
the precipitous troughs and channels
of her flanks, haunches and legs—all suggest

the complexities of a primal epoch,
the immensities of unexplored tundra.
My three colleagues and I take our stand
together. One of us presents her with
a tall book: our proclamations,

our desire to be confirmed in our explanations
of the hand and the fingernail, the face,
the warp and woof of the sky, the necklaces
of words wrapped around our hearts
and throats, the texture of a wing feather,

the universe in a drop of sacrificial blood.
She tilts her head, the grey gates of her ears
swinging on their hinges. One of us
holds out a band of cloth strung
with bells, reverberation among

the wind-scoured walls and towers,
a banishment of silence. She blinks,
lets go a mammoth chuff of breath.
Jingling does not charm her.
One of us spreads his arms in prayer,

casting hopeful side-long glances her way,
imploring her for forgiveness, though
our clarity about sin flew with the last
flocks of southbound starlings and juncos.
She curls her trunk as if speaking to herself,

the white mouth at the end open wide
in small guffaw. I turn my face to the sky
and sing, praising the muscularity
of her thighs, the darkness of her underbelly,
the delicate enormity of her extended tail.

The customary authority of my voice shatters,
shards scrambling like scorpions into gullies.
A small white face peers from the convoluted
warren of her ear, its speech too soft for us to hear.
She uproots one foot and takes an enormous step

closer, continental drift, and the four of us
draw together to make our last stand.
Curious, she only wants to study our text,
perfected scrawl, like the scratches
on stone or tree-trunk she makes with her behind.

FLESH AMONG THE FERNS

Love Song of the Maintenance Engineer

      1.

my life drains like dirty water
into the windows I wash
into the endless hardwood floor
of the hall I mop clean as a flame

the minutes slink into doors one by one
sink their claws into white plaster walls
stupid cicadas

until I see you
my new assistant
laughing your black bag down the halls
spinning jazz-steps into vacant offices
waltzing into the dawn light
that falls like tablecloth onto classroom desks
and your minutes together with mine
drop into the clusters of dust
and you sweep them all away

      2.

I float in a white hammock
on my day off waiting for you
trees above me swing nothing in their heads
nothing that flows like river through weeds
nothing that curls into lip and word

the shade of these old oaks fails me
I look through the sweaty mask of my hands
at the rifts of leaves and limbs

the brown grass beneath me
gathering and holding the heat of the day
exhausted from wanting you
I can't think of tv or movies
I must sleep for hours
and when I wake
the night will be something comfortable
you slip into

    3.
last night's whispers are now your words
wrapping my super's voice with white paper
and saying keep your eyes on the floor
on the mop on the bucket of water
on the trashcans full of forgotten sentences
on the trees outside that mark the falling of time

the old wishes dance in our veins
I watch your thin body bend into lifting
like a bird before it leaps into flight
like the lull before the high note of your favorite song
the keys to every door slap our thighs
we have filled-out the same forms
cleaned the same rooms
you and I

    4.
kiss me and I'll dream for a thousand years
I'll follow your breath the way it turns against my face
I'll never speak of money or of cars with electric windows
I'll never hold myself up to anyone's light but yours
I'll follow the sparrow's call into the woods

I'll listen to the wind in every kind of tree
in the river of our valley of night I'll speak the first words
which cannot be planned or cancelled
you know the ones

      5.
in the dawn all your roses rhyme
I believe the trees belong to no one
except those small homeowners
flickering among the boughs

another night another day another
gallery of glances among the sheets and windows
and no one not even you my love
can say what is happening
though you speak for ten thousand years

      6.
we stop to speak to a dog
who has taken root in the rain
mumbling under its soggy breath
about the ground it must guard

the next day there is sun
and the dog sleeps on a porch

mind too full of its days like us
it dreams of that moment
when from the tall weeds beyond fences
the hare emerges
coat full of the scent
of chase and escape

      7.
didn't see you last night
didn't find your face in the pillows
didn't listen to your voice
filling that space between day and dream
didn't discover your hand on my thigh
searching for the key I will never possess
what I mean to say
is that the streets are longer than ever
continue in fact around the world
if you count the paths of planes and ships
and I know you want to go somewhere

I stare at an old man on the street
pushing a wheelchair loaded
with black bags strapped in by ropes
what's the difference between me and him
looking everywhere
in newspaper machines for coins
in trashcans for bottles
everywhere is the key
for what is valuable
never stopping for long
how can anything be important

      8.
and I would've gone someplace too
but I didn't
is it different in Chicago or St. Louis
or some small town in South Dakota
or wherever you are
in the valley of your faraway night

even farther away in a deep silence the satellite
catches info and spits it back
to the dish we splurged on together
so I can sit here alone on my couch
on the one day that's mine
and decide to watch a program
about the Klan in Georgia

a grinning wizard
the murder of a black man
the burning of a famous Jew in effigy

I make another tv decision
that you wouldn't like if you were here
and a bulldog mascot
slobbers on the sideline
beside the fat calf muscle of a fullback
the crowd screams and a flag
the size of a continent

unfurls over the stadium where the great clock
burns each huge white second into my brain

Lust at the Lecture on Modernist Painters

1. Arrival

Body as cloud
drifting through trees,
cloud as body
morphing in the high winds.

I arrive late
and the people I know
lock elbow to elbow
within their rows.
I find a seat
next to a student,
naked feet and toe rings,
fingernails and toenails glowing blue.
Now how am I
supposed to hear the scholars
explore the transformations
of four modernists turned expressionists
sitting next to those jubilant toes?

On the screen
a long skinny hairy bodiless arm
reaches from some exterior dimension
into the still life landscape
of a room—a chair, a table, a cup
of coffee with a tuft of steam—
a unified sense of presence
and absence.

2. The Lecture

the garland of bones
the gnarled feet of gnomes
the vegetable demon
chameleons in the corn
the foil of gusts
the sheen of morning water
chiaroscuro of a room
drama of the object frankly stellar
the vehicle of a dream
the bifurcation of smoke rings
instances of disconnection
instances of interface
the broken stroke
riding a wild image
the threshold of a drama
the modifications of motif
half organic half metallic
beyond the interplay of surface
a dissatisfaction with the containing edge
a thing in a place
a place containing things
drunken brush drunken line
drunken rain on the window
bring the hand back in
let it languish on the table
the face that is not a face
foot floating above a mattress
mouth spitting out a gold ring
the twisted torso
among the twisted sheets

evidence of desire
content is a slippery glimpse
an admiration of naked kneecaps
evidence of the incomplete motive
toe-rings on slender toes
a notion of where things fit
the out of phase phase
the biases of the eye
the call of the unknown within the known

    3. Interlude

The evidence of a body
is a door
creaking open on its hinges
as if by wind,
is the hollowness
of the hallway in moonlight
or in sunlight on gray rainy days,
is the loveliness of knees
pressed together beside me—
the heaviness of walls.

    4. Serious Daydream

All of us, each of us, unaware
of the genetic possibility, the potential
in the biological scheme that we are—
Lopez unaware, on the Antarctic tundra,
the last great glacier's blue receding
into white beneath his eyes—

not the blue of toenails
redefining blue for all time—

Williams unaware, among the burrowing owls,
the whimbrells, disappearing
from the marsh—

I, unaware of the great earth spinning
down my spine, a vortex of energy
pouring into my bones—feeling only
the long bone of a thigh
against the long bone of my own.

Constellations of the city
spiral in the curved distance,
consuming darkness but only for a time,
everything only for a time, darkness
a given that cannot be finally consumed—

unless it's the darkness of eyes,
then the flash of blue lids closing,
then the embodied darkness lying down again.

Imagine a mutation in the DNA
that transcends predator/prey
economics, sexual gratification
consumerism—

the blue of painted toes,
the rose of lips…

5. Afterwards

She nibbled on cheese and crackers,
the luminous blue of her nails
shimmering against the red wine.

Then she disappeared,
the cloud of a body
making its long journey
into the bodies of clouds.

Later, I lay down in a meadow
surrounded by woods, and allowed
the shadows among the leaves of oak and birch
to grow together in full darkness around me.
The night voices rose up in scattered song.
I have seen enough of this world
to know what I love—paintings
that show me how to see
what I haven't seen: a young woman
I don't know with rings on her toes;
the earth bearing me
through space, spinning
on its own center and circling the sun,
manifesting me as this flesh among the ferns.

Nameable Strangers

Second Sight

Into this walking I retired a year ago.
A fist of cumulus gathers up the moon.
A man presses his forehead to a wall,
a woman lies down beneath a window
hoping for some freshness on her skin.
Balanced on the heads of sleeping children,
ghosts of men who chewed their own knuckles
for a hundred years, of women who left
the doors open far into every fall.
My wife was one of them.

Nothing is left to coincidence
but to threadbare words hung out on the line each day.
Believers gather to worship a manifestation of Jesus
in shadows that play on the pharmacy wall.
How my wife would have laughed.

I did not come here by choice,
but my mother carried me slung under her arm.
Then I rode on my father's head like a crown—
a pair of elevated eyes training in the art of second sight.

Now I'm lucky to find my shoes under the couch
where cats have gnawed the laces.
I step into the new day spitting the minutes out like seeds.
She with her busy hands would not have approved.
Cracks and potholes accumulate under the sun.
The days are no more dangerous than dogs.
The theater reopens with a string of B movies.

Boys throng in vacant lots and abandoned houses.
Girls laugh from windows.
My neighbor plays saxophone every afternoon
the way my wife used to like it.

The river cuts out another yard of clay in the spring.
I refuse to budge, I walk my route
like some old tractor in a fallow pasture.
My cousin in Atlanta has given up on me.
I listen to country songs full of lost women.
Under the tree that her great-grandmother planted
she sat in a chair I made for her.
She was too tired to speak by then,
just gazed at her street until the months
turned into days and the days into hours—
the hours into the last breezy leaves above her.

Trouble

A huge eagle landed
in the soccer field today.
The boys said its eyes
shot purple balls of fire
and they ran, but couldn't
wash the stains from their dreams.
The girls stood their ground,
drawing magenta into the bottomless
pools of their brains,
into the white-throated
sparrows of their hearts.
The eagle presented
each girl a feather the size
of a door, and each embraced
her feather in that shy dance.
People from the neighborhood
gathered to watch.
When the eagle lifted off
throwing a monumental
shadow over the town,
the girls lay down
in the grass with their tall,
sleek feathers and gazed
at the fading sky. The people
could not get them to move
and had to carry them
with their feathers like wounded
birds back to their beds

in the dimly lit houses.
That night the feathers
gathered light from the moon
through open windows,
and the next morning
the girls awoke
shining in their new bodies,
ready for their featherless flight.

The Vein in a Child's Temple

In the circle of men, Frank
snaps the next card down,
yawning, unconcerned with loss.
He thinks of that blue vein
in his small daughter's temple,
thinks of her mild pulse. The bet's

too steep for his pair of eights.
He drops his cards, finishes off
the last ounce of a warm beer,
laughs on his way out at a joke
that places him with the wiry waitress
at the Waffle House on highway 9.

Outside, the tiny skull of a robin
looks like a pale gray leaf
twisted by wind and gully-washers.
Darkness comes soon enough
and the white river tosses
its last knives into distant hills.

It's hard to say no to these men
whose talk is about the half-ass lumber
from Graves Mill lately, whose hands
are cracked and swollen as his
from a long day of putting down shingles.
A little drunk, Frank gets lost

on the short-cut home.
In the labyrinth of back alleys
and tree-lined ditches, he thinks
of his wife Emma, an old-fashioned name
even in Virginia, her face beautiful in no way
a young man could acknowledge.

He thinks of the dinner she's put away by now
but will bring back out for him:
maybe ham, maybe black-eyed peas.
He savors the thought of her hands
like sunlight, like dusk, like everything
warm that settles onto low places.

One of Us

Here in Montana, the streets touch horizon,
shimmer with mirage. The bear
in the backyard cage is painfully

mute, more one of us than not.
The lodge owner slides pans
of venison and berries under

the gate. Twenty years ago he left
his wife and daughters in Detroit.
Behind his ornately carved bar,

he tells of a species of blind
rats living in the sewers of the city, forepaws
like the hands of a human fetus.

Their clammy touch awakens
the fires of vision in any sleeper.
Next day one's memories have

become dreams free-falling
into darkness. Thus his wife
forgot him, he says, and still wanders

the dangerous streets looking
for nameable strangers. Once, however,
we found the owner lying next

to his bear in the cage, whispering,
"Michele, come back to me." We wonder
among ourselves who it is that was

touched by the rat's claw, and who
it is that slips peacefully between
the sheets on a summer's night.

The Prisoner's Dance

I twist a piece, warm and heavy, from the loaf.
Outside my window, a wren that would fit neatly
in my floating palm, detaches a seed from the feeder

and flits to a bobbing limb of the red bud tree. I remember
the night I would not dance among strangers, even though

her eyes beckoned me to the floor where she stood alone
among the others gathering to the prison of the music.
That's what I called it then in my mind, not understanding

the oiled precision of my own cell. The wren crouches
briefly and uncoils into the air—does she catch it? or it, her—

where nothing like hope is required. Only weightless feathers
and hollow bones, the desire to leap and fall and swoon,
and blood so quick and light it ends in song. I wrap the bread

in foil and raise my heavy bones from their solid perch.
If I could cradle a willing wren in my hands and carry it

as a gift to the woman standing alone in the yard
speaking in mysterious tongues to the trees she planted,
I know she would shake her head at me and send it

flying on its way. Instead, I quickstep across the threshold
like an old but agile crow. So liberating, now, how she watches me.

Your Eyes When You Walk Out on Me

are like the early light
slashing through maple leaves.
Like a window left open
to let the flying insects in
on a clear windy night.
Like your vacancy-sign hand
pressing on the center
of my chest, or crumpling
the dead pack of cigarettes.
Like a thrown fist
reaching the end of its arm
in empty air.
Like a leaf broken off
by the wind, falling,
flying wild over the blacktop.
Like a rock thrown
straight down into the pond,
small mushroom cloud rising
into the current.
Like a swollen river in moonlight.

Like moon-shards scattered
over the mowed lawn
while I lie awake in this vast room.
Like a spider on the wall
that is only a small smudge
till it strikes.
Like a door in that wall
that leads to a room

full of an empty bed
and the silence gathering
to call you back.
Like your hand wrapped
around a key in a pocket
when you return to me.
Like the skein of your voice
unraveling its yellow yarn on the floor.
Like the story you don't tell me
when you are telling me your story
in the razor-light of morning.

Woodcreek 1977
for Harriet

A golden retriever named Jason
lies in a pile of red and yellow leaves,
dark eyes ready for more play,
one front paw nonchalantly draped over the other,
such happiness penetrating us like air.

A friend loaned us her summer house that winter,
a poorly built fireplace in the main room
all we had for heat, naïve portraits
of the family's long dead horses
all we had for art. The only way to find us
was the long furrow of a road among slash pine.
Nobody came. The moonlight played
in a million spoons on the lake.
The old fishing boat kept untying itself,
drifting out from the ancient boathouse
like a dead leaf.

We are their voices:
the ones who paddled at midnight
among the nibbling bream,
who came flying drunk
down the backwoods macadam
on that leaky old motorcycle
held together with green cord and duct tape.

Today I put my ear to the ground and hear
our bodies careening through the underbrush
of that long ago night

while the motorcycle spins around on its footpeg
and chokes on sand.

Remember this with me
—you who were there
and are here—
the way we lay flat under that pale night sky
scraped and bruised among the scrub oak
laughing at the silence,
laughing at our own dumb luck.

Asleep

     1.
It is always the same hotel.
Your breathing is a wind high in the trees,
only the touch of its feathery tail
sliding over my face. Your sleep-voice
mumbles and says nothing.

But here and now, a small tree grows
under the house, its first limbs learning
to lie back like palms.
In the night-windows I see my reflection:
old man drinking from a brown sack;
small boy trying to force his face
through a crack in the door.

     2.
Gone is the moon with its small bright voice.
Gone is the day with its plans for the next excavation.
Gone are the eyes that open like a hillside field,
the face that enters the tall grass emerging
again and again, never the same. Gone
is your name. I have buried the feet
of those beautiful days in the garden. The skies
of those nights ride the backs of distant clouds.

     3.
Say hello to the stars that keep up
their screeching like teenagers in a park.
Say hello to that ugly pair of shoes

that have lurked under the bureau for years.
Say hello to the small spider
that leaps over the gulches and cliffs of my shirt
searching for something smaller and alive.
Say hello to the parking lot grown empty
in the afternoon with the sun bearing down
into the few remaining windshields,
to the hot breeze gusting low over buildings,
dropping into trees where the leaves cannot
control themselves. Say hello to the brick
facades with their serious faces, to the people
walking in and out calling each other
by the names they have earned. I want to say
your name over and over but can't without
stopping first, your name that stumbles
onto my tongue ahead of all others,
impediment to greetings. Say hello to no sign
of you anywhere for weeks then months on end.

    4.
I have given up on the idea of not thinking.
Mantras, meditation, prayer cannot make it happen.
Send directions. Give me some signal.
In the middle of the night, in the middle
of a dream about people I'm supposed to know
gathering at a beach hotel, you appear, taking
note of me with a glance, you whose eyes are always
changing under those uncertain lights swaying
in the warm wind off the ocean. Why do you watch
the bobbing hands of that small man with a red beard
who seems able to talk forever? He takes you

by the wrist and leads you away.
Why do you look over your shoulder at me
for that brief moment, not quite turning —
and me, only a dim speck in the distance
away from the lights, down by the water
with the tide going out, my feet disappearing
in the liquid sand, and behind me
that flame of moon beyond the breakers?

Near

Under the old moon a red dog lopes,
heading toward the one dear face,
the one pair of hands smelling
of cinnamon and roots.
There is nothing old
under the old moon,
nothing wounded or torn
under the restraint
of its reflected light,
everything mended or emerging.
My feet, for example, on the bed, gleaming
like carved pine under the window.
The cheap copper ring
I bought at the carnival last year
glows—horse's eye
in midnight darkness.
It may take me another hour
of simmering in that deep well
of original but angled light
to awaken to your new face
that I have known these forty years.
Your body is a shining pool
stretched out under that same moon.
Tomorrow many will watch as you ride
a great bay horse called Echo.
But for now our dreams have boiled
and burned away into mist.
We are as near to nothing as anything
under the morning sky.
We are as near to new.

Things Would Be Different: An Aubade to My Cat
for Harriet

Congratulations, Yoda, oh wise one.
You have peppered my pillow with hair,
you have turned my belly
into your pedestal
upon which you lie
poised on the verge of a riddle
until you stand and stretch,
putting another notch on my navel
with those retractable claws
you never retract.
And when I turn over
to bury my head under covers
you stay balanced and afloat like a logger
turning a great tree trunk beneath your feet
indifferent to dangerous waters
churning past.
There is much I can learn from you
enlightened one
before I even leave my morning bed:
the way you freshen your cold, fish-foul teeth
against my beard,
the way the hooks and loops of your tongue
scrape the hairy top-skin of my fingers raw.
Who else could get away with these indignities
and live?
Not Obi Wan Kinobe,
nor Darth Vader himself.
I salute you queen of the night crawlers,
princess of the bed burrowers,
lying low now against my naked leg,
that small motor turning prime salmon and tuna

into lumpy, pink constellations on the carpet.
Were it not for the woman
whose snores envelop the lake of chaos like mist,
whose languorous limbs are the map of my desire,
who loves every manifestation of catness,
oblivious to my stifled protestations,
allowing all manner of malignant feline design
like kneading my thigh under the sheets,
like preening on the windowsills
to the stark terror of chickadees and white-throated sparrows,
like grooming on the mantel among the busts and vases,
yes, even ass-licking among the stacked dishes,
primping among the cleansers and sponges
in the cavernous darkness of cabinets
whose doors pop open whenever you appear—
yes, were it not for her whose touch
conjures all sense of well-being,
whose music invokes laughter and joy,
you would be dancing to a different tune,
black usurper of hearth and couch,
rotund belly-up snuggler among the cushions,
you peddler of cuteness and acrobatic sideshows,
nothing could save you,
not even the mangled carcasses of mouse and mole
presented neatly on the front stoop,
not even the well-placed colons and semi-colons
of your hairballs,
though I appreciate good punctuation
as much as the next fellow.
Yes, my midnight yodeler from the chest of drawers,
my flea-flicking follicle-licking friend,
my invulnerable Yoda smiling from the foot of the bed,
things would be different around here
were it not for this woman asleep beside me.

Original Face

With a stick of chalk leftover
from his years of teaching, an old man
draws a face on the gray cement floor,
anonymous, poised to speak.
The old man talks to its half-open eyes
about the state of his affairs—
the small room with a toilet and a hotplate
in a building that should be condemned.

He dances on the face, smears its eyes,
the mouth agape like a clown's—
his own face, he thinks, before he was born.
He scoops the face up with his hat
and snaps it down on his head,
no longer asking himself how such things
occur in a world of hard facts.
He exits via his fire escape,
drops like a gymnast to the rain-soaked
concrete of the alley. He crouches,
feels his bones stunned
like tuning forks within his flesh.

He walks, and the face in his hat
does not know the trees—"cherry,"
the old man says—nor does it know
the flowers—"marigolds, buttercups."
The face in the old man's hat
does not know the names of streets —
"Rivermont, Princeton," the old man says.

Two children are aping sex
between the grill and bumper of parked cars.
"Love," the old man says.
The face in his hat replies, "No wonder
you are still living alone." In the park
the face says, "I'll show you something
you have never seen." The old man
laughs, says, "Face, I have
created you. You can't show me anything."

The old man comes upon a woman
lying in a patch of grass beneath Chinaberry trees.
"Is this what you mean?" he asks.
"Yes," says the face.
The old man introduces himself, bows,
drops his hat on the grass, and the face
steals away into roots, rises into leaves
flipping their pale undersides to the sky,
hovers like an early moon among the limbs.
The woman asks the old man to join her
in a crossword puzzle. He settles beside her
on her blanket. Her fine, old hands move
over the half-formed words.

Later, back in his own room,
he catches himself laughing
as he flips a cheese sandwich
onto the hotplate sizzling with butter.
He flips it again, making it tumble
three times in the air, and her laugh
draws the day's last low sunlight

through the window
where the face lingers, a disc
of shadow shifting into dusk.

The old man counts ten slow seconds
and sneaks another look at her,
her immaculate hands cupped
one inside the other in her lap,
her paper folded neatly, tucked inside
her purse on the floor. The stranger
came home with him
in her green cardigan sweater,

her trust so frightening his hands
have not stopped shaking. His original face....
shining now...from within her face.

Down and Up

For a while he frequented a certain
bar, but it was only talk, only sex.
Then he just started heading
straight for home after a day
spinning in his office chair
among the keyboards and screens.
He'd hit the TV power button
to keep the world jumping in
with faces pretending to know,
voices tuned to heartfelt emotion.
His nightly routine: cook the meal
he'd planned, watch the recommended
movie, and so on. But then he started
ignoring the characters and the story,
more taken by the flickering hues
on the wall. And then not even that,
just sat down in that dark room
where the blinds allow street light
to skip from the rolltop desk
to the slatted back of the wooden chair
to the dim gray of the mirror
where his face shifted personalities
like x-ray vision through a deck of cards.
He wanted to see all of the faces he'd ever
lived: crumpled brow to smooth facade,
high cheek bones to double chin,
tight thin lips to toothy smirk,
narrowed eyes of knowing to love-gaze.
There was no one to stop him now—

parents dead, ex-wife long ago gone
into her garden and another man's child.
No one to encourage him either.
Beyond the last face in the mirror
lurked a gallery of long-gone countenances
he couldn't reach. That's when he dug out
the old lawn chair, lugged it down
those five flights of stairs, going deeper
into the mystery as if some hypnotherapist
guided him down that switchbacking
stair well, the chipped paint of the hand rail
cracking beneath his fingers, the yellow
light of the bracketed bulbs creeping down

the wall ahead of him, the reverberation
of his footfalls sounding the depths
where his neighbors slept or made love
or drifted in their drug-induced dreams,
to this comfy location for his lawn chair
blocked from street-view by the dumpster.
He liked the dampness there, liked
his holey sweater to keep away the chill,
liked the way bars of moonlight and starlight
bending through slats of the fire escape
crawled along the alley wall like fingers
getting to know a face. The gang
of his ancient countenances careened
within the luster of that cold, forgiving light,
until the first one loomed before him—
featureless, speechless, shining, shining.

    * * *

His keys jingle with a jovial warmth
against his thigh. He climbs, slowly,
higher and higher in the stairwell,
opens the door of his own rooms,
leans in as if he's never seen them before.
Looks out his unadorned windows
through his own phantom reflection
onto this town strewn with lights.
What made him think it wasn't good
just to be here, each light out there
an individual room, a universe of states
of mind. He opens himself a can of tuna,
drinks a beer, takes note of his car keys
on the counter. He can leave if he wants to,
get behind the wheel of his old Grand Am
and drive until it dies in some desert
or at least until he finds a good reason
to gather the world around himself again,
some reason to form a new and distinct face.
He can take his time, can stay here all night, all week,
all month…the rest of his life if he wants.

The Grip
  for my mother

The oxygen machine shoots out another puff,
and my mother takes another breath
from the tube in her nose. Her eyes open,
a subtle smile rising in her resigned face
when she sees me. The TV flickers
and she straightens up in her recliner
to watch her favorite macho crime buster—

Chuck Norris—pursue a slick, black-
suited, thug-protected, drug lord this time.
But her eyes wander, and she doesn't see
Chuck whirl another karate kick to a hooligan head.
Instead, her eyes come to rest on the clown
puppet astride the top shelf of her bookcase.
She doesn't dwell on the overlarge

red smile, the blue exclamatory eyes.
Instead, her eyes turn inward to the scene
she has described to me many times before:
the arthritic hands of the shopkeeper
rake the puppet down from a display
and set it vividly upright on the counter—
that brash splash of color and gangly cloth—

and my mother reaches into its body
for the hidden grip, makes its wooden shoes
dance on the counter, makes its stuffed head
bob to a tune she sings, and the gap-toothed
old shopkeeper claps and laughs.

As a kid of five, I'd run into my parents' room,
pull that jester down and find the inner

grip, make it dance, make it tell the jokes
I'd heard my mother tell but didn't
understand, make it sing to the dog
who'd run and hide behind the couch
wild-eyed until she placed the puppet back
on its perch. From her mother dimension
high among the fluorescent lights, she

coached me through the solar system of house,
over thresholds into the galaxy of backyard,
through the gate into the universe of town and beyond.
My mother's eyes surface to the here and now,
pass over the credits rising on the TV screen,
settle on my face. Her dying eyes find my living eyes—
take hold, gently, of the well-worn grip inside.

Las Vegas
for my father

Your hand opens
over my face
like a spider parachuting
on its thread
to living stone.
Not a spider after all
but fingers so gentle
the tiny hairs on my brow
rise up to bridge the gap,
my head waking from stone
into the bone of touch.
An old movie flickers,
faintly mumbles on the TV,
and the Casablanca of my heart
opens too, to mysterious
strangers and acts of unexpected
kindness. Did you long
to close up your offices,
board up the windows and doors,
and ignore the faces in passing cars
that knew you like the names
of their own streets?
Did you long to travel to some far place
where the women you dreamed of
turned their sly eyes in your direction
in the midst of a drink, a conversation?
The promise is almost as good as the gift itself.
You are long gone into the earth
of a green hill, and yet

you turn to me now, you
who traveled only so far
as Las Vegas, and shake
your head, saying,
hush, hush, go to sleep.

The Note

A slip of paper tumbles down the street
ahead of me. I can make out writing
but I can't read it because it twists
in the wind, a piece torn from a full sheet
with small scribbling and a signature.
I want to know what it says, though I'm sure
it's a note for someone else. Maybe for the man
on my street who wears his coat inside out
when he's walking in the June rain.
He lights the filter end of his cigarette
and presents it to a woman who backs away
slowly, then dances with his right shoe
on his left foot and his left shoe on his right foot
at the grand opening of the furniture store.
He frowns at a good joke and laughs at the deaths
of his friend's wife and children in an accident,
and later prays to his descendants generations off
to send him a map or a hint or a good dream.
He sleeps the heart of the day away and walks
wide-eyed all night through city streets.
Maybe the note tells him it's okay to stay reversed.
Or maybe it says, no man who holds faithfully
to his backward ways shall be denied a ticket
to the ball park. Strangers sit next to him
in the right field seats hoping for homers.

Maybe the note is for the woman I see on the bus
who talks to herself all day, her hands
sprouting around her head, her eyes flitting
from face to face, her feet in red

ankle-top Converse Allstars dancing
beneath her seat, flashing her white socks
beneath the flourish of a flouncy blue skirt,
her voice full of parentheses and dashes,
unwinding as smooth as shifting gears with no
top end, pleading to her son who wrote a book
about a boy whose mother never stops
talking, to her husband who fled
on the night of their seventh anniversary
in a rented tux and carrying a green bottle,
to the social worker who keeps an eye on her,
though she never takes her for pizza, or calls her
on Sunday morning like a daughter should.
Maybe the note tells her to keep on talking.
After all, it's gotten her this far. Or maybe
it tells her if she's quiet for one whole
minute, she will awaken to a sound
on the other side of her eternal voice
that allows the space around her to relax
so that the next boy that gets on the bus
sits near her and asks her where the hell
did she get those red Allstars.

Or maybe the note is for me since I'm
the one who sees it. Do I have to be logical
all the time? Maybe it's a note from my father
who never finished high school, instead
taught himself to agent insurance
and later to build and sell houses
and to draw plans as well as an architect,
who punched out any man who looked
at my mother for more than two seconds,

who promoted fights where black men
fought white men in a smoke-filled arena,
who made too damn much money and never knew
what he wanted or what he was living for.
So what would he say in that note? Maybe
to stay away from dangerous women.

Or maybe it's a note from my mother
who liked the way my father protected her,
who gave birth to me just to prove to him
she could make a boy who would grow up to be a man.
Maybe her note tells me she wants to be a courtesan
in her next life, or a happy loose woman anyway.

The Syllable

I always wondered if I were born
of a secret syllable—
my mother the vowel, my father the consonant—
spoken in the first entanglements of dawn
or the dramatic dissipations of dusk,
spoken even now on the undersides of leaves,
on the undersides of stones in dried-up creek beds.

And now as I become one who speaks,
mother vowel and father consonant
rouse their ancient enmity and lust
within some whirligig repository
of possible thought and word.

I stand and sit among my own kind
and the words collect like birds
in the canopy of my brain
where they wait for the moment
of self-projection to materialize,
finally to fly
from the windblown limb of my tongue.

Is this just me playing
the word-game of myself?
Words grow into phrases and clauses
and full-blown sentences—paragraphs
and essays and diatribes, sermons and rants
and desperate pleading in the night—
Vowel Eve, Consonant Adam, constantly
conceiving the old and the new within me.

Epilogue:
Migration

A vase half full of dirty water gathers light
on a windowsill in a house surrounded
by forest on a piece of forgotten land.
A book on the sill opens under the open window.
Breezes flip its pages until each leaf
has its own moment in the sunlight or in

cold shadow, letters long gone,
lifted off to become particles of air.
Clothes made for a man and a woman hang
on a line stretched between two trees so old
their voices uncoil from roots that plunge
into earth's core and soar from the highest branch

to track the faraway scars of starlight.
The words in towns and cities resonate
and tear themselves from books
like a swarm of ants that crawl over miles
and miles of undergrowth and roots
and ancient deer trails and up the exterior wall

of this house. They fill the emptiness
of the book's pages beside the vase
where their meanings surge and coalesce
in the candlelit attentions of the man and woman.
Sometimes the words form a choir and sing:
here are the seeds of new understanding

untouched by the past; here are the bodies
of a man and a woman entangled under the sweet
verbosity of leaves; here is the place where
something in the muddy water germinates,
concentrates like a face. The moon grows full
and round as the woman. The man sleeps

open-mouthed in the sun.

About the Poet

Jim Peterson was born in Georgia and grew up in South Carolina. His B.A., M.A., and Ph.D. are all in English and from the University of South Carolina. He has published four previous full-length collections of poetry—*The Man Who Grew Silent* (The Bench Press 1989), *An Afternoon With K* (Holocene 1996), *The Owning Stone* (Red Hen Press 2000 and 2011), and *The Bob and Weave* (Red Hen 2006)—and a novel, *Paper Crown* (Red Hen 2005). Over the years, three chapbooks of his poems have appeared: *Carvings on a Prayer Tree*, *Greatest Hits 1984-2000*, and *The Resolution of Eve*. His poems have appeared in more than seventy journals including *Poetry*, *Georgia Review*, *Shenandoah*, *Poetry Northwest*, *Prairie Schooner*, *Cave Wall*, *South Dakota Review*, and *Connecticut Review,* and have won the Benjamin Saltman Award from Red Hen Press, an Academy of American Poets Award, and a Fellowship in Poetry from the Virginia Arts Commission. His plays have been produced in college and regional theatres. He is on the faculty of the University of Nebraska MFA Program in Creative Writing, and he recently retired as Coordinator of Creative Writing/Writer in Residence at Randolph College in Lynchburg, Virginia. He lives in Lynchburg with his amazing wife Harriet and their charismatic Welsh Corgi, Mama Kilya.

CPSIA information can be obtained at www.ICGtesting.com
Printed in the USA
BVOW08s2303061015
421295BV00003B/59/P